HABITS AND HAPPINESS

How to Become Happier and
Improve Your Wellbeing by
Changing Your Habits

D1359464

Braco Pobric

High Impact Consulting, LLC
Publishing Division
Mercerville, NJ
P.O. Box 2596

ISBN-13: 978-1493662456

ISBN-10: 1493662457

Library of Congress Control Number: 201491014

CreateSpace Independent Publishing Platform
North Charleston, SC

Ordering Information:
Quantity sales. Special discounts are available on quantity purchases by corporations, associations, and others. For details, contact the publisher at the address above.

Printed in the United States of America

HABITS AND HAPPINESS

How to Become Happier and Improve Your Wellbeing by Changing Your Habits

"In this brief, practical, and important book, Braco Pobric offers a blueprint for bringing about positive change in your life. Read it and, more importantly, apply it!"

– Tal Ben Shahar, PhD, author of the international bestsellers *Happier* and *Being Happy*

"*Habits and Happiness* importantly reminds us that, scientifically, happiness can be a choice if we change our behavior. Pobric creates a great link between research and practice in our daily lives."

– Shawn Achor, New York Times bestselling author of the *Happiness Advantage and Before Happiness*

"We all have habits we want to change, but how do we do it? Thanks to Braco Pobric we now have a simple, prescriptive path. Habits and Happiness is rich with stories and examples everyone can identify with. Use this delightful and effective book to enhance the happiness and results of yourself, your team, your family."

– Christine Comaford, Leadership and Culture Coach, New York Times bestselling author of *Smart Tribes: How Teams Become Brilliant Together*

"There are few books that stress the importance of dedicated work when it comes to habits and happiness. I applaud Braco Pobric for having the insight and the courage to do so in his well-researched and compassionately written book. I am sure that it will help many to instigate lasting change."

– Andrea F. Polard, PsyD, author of *A Unified Theory of Happiness: An East-Meets-West Approach to Fully Loving Your Life*

The Buddha said all things change. They do not, however, always change for the better. Yet by harnessing the incredible power of virtuous habits, the inevitable transformations we experience can become more wholesome, and hence we can become happier people. In this elegant, practical, and scientifically grounded book, Braco Pobric shows us the many ways skillful change is possible in every area of our lives. We are changing anyway; why not make it for the better?

– Mark W. Muesse, W.J. Millard Professor of Religious Studies, Rhodes College, author of *Practicing Mindfulness*

"Bad habits, vices, problem behaviors, 7 deadly sins, low energy, vicious circles, poor motivation. These are problems and patterns all of us face to one degree or another. The good news is we can transform, manage, and transcend many of these phenomena.

In Habits and Happiness, Braco Pobric shifts the conversation to a conscious focus on cultivating healthy, positive, and substantial habits that we can sustain.

Braco's approach is a practical one, rooted in positive psychology principles and research. Adhering to these ideas will help you make those vexing behavioral changes you have been wanting to make but in a way you perhaps had never thought of.

The result? Most likely: greater happiness, health, and overall well-being."

– Ryan M. Niemiec, PsyD, author of several books, including *Mindfulness and Character Strengths*: A *Practical Guide to Flourishing*; and *Education Director, VIA Institute on Character*

"Scientists who study happiness have conducted hundreds of brilliant scientific studies (many of which are summarized in this book), yet scientists rarely communicate their findings to the general public in an accessible manner. In this book, Braco Pobric picks up where scientists left off and provides an outstanding tutorial on the practical application of scientific research to change habits and increase happiness."

– Chad Burton, PhD, Social Scientist

"Happiness, health, wellbeing, productivity, meaning—we all long for increases in each of these arenas at various times, yet longing is never enough. Thinking about change is not enough. Talking about change changes nothing. We must actually take the steps to change habits that inhibit our forward movement and choose instead habits that potentiate our growth. This book, direct, clear and encouraging, cuts to the essence of successful habit formation...and it is through this formation that we grow. Anyone who is ready to craft a life that is richer, healthier and happier, will find the tools in this book to do so."

– Dr. Maria Sirois, author of *Every Day Counts: Lessons in Love, Faith, and Resilience from Children Facing Illness*

"Braco Pobric's *Habits and Happiness* is an inspiring and informative book. One can find motivation in Braco's personal experience of habits and through his offering of the research concerning how habits are formed and how they support or harm us. The book also provides ideas of useful habits we can all implement and practical steps towards forming and maintaining them."

– Deborah R. Cohen, MAPP, author of *Journey to Inner Space: A Children's Yoga Book*

To Nevenka, my love

CONTENTS

**We are what we repeatedly do.
Excellence then, is not an act, but a habit.**

— Aristotle

PREFACE

This book is intended to help you understand how habits work, and will also give you practical examples as a way to introduce new habits into your life. It is my hope that, at the very least, you will find the information presented here helpful, challenging, and motivating in developing your own new habits.

Implementing habitual behavior in accordance with this book will help you become happier and more successful, will improve your wellbeing, and will assist you to live the life you've always wanted to live.

We can learn so much about ourselves by learning about our habits. Our wellbeing increases significantly when we understand the reasons we do certain things, when we learn how to change and introduce new habits if necessary, and when we apply that knowledge effectively in our lives.

My goal is not to present a scientific research paper that few will understand, but rather to help you improve your wellbeing by introducing *good* new habits and changing *bad* old habits. At the same time I will provide the research supporting these ideas.

Please note that I am not a licensed psychologist, neuroscientist, psychiatrist, psychotherapist, nor a medical doctor, and the material in this book is not professional medical or psychological advice. If you need help in those areas, please consult a certified and licensed professional.

When we look at living creatures from an outward point of view, one of the first things that strike us is that they are bundles of habits.

—William James

INTRODUCTION

Before I can tell you anything about habits, I must first acknowledge the work of William James, often referred to as the father of American psychology, who dedicated a great portion of his work to the study of habits. Although his research was done in the late 1800s and early 1900s (he died in 1910) he provided the fundamental principles that are the basis for habit studies. Not only that, but what he knew more than 100 years ago, science proves today.

"If one has not taken advantage of every concrete opportunity to act," William James once wrote, "one's character may remain entirely unaffected for the better."

While it is important that you grasp and fully understand the theory and knowledge presented here, be aware that this alone will change nothing in your life. You will have to work in order to make this happen.

Before you continue reading, make sure you are committed to implementing the knowledge learned here, otherwise your experience will be the same as with many other books you may have read, and nothing will change. *This is because reading alone will not change a behavior.* For change to occur, you must be committed. Then you have to follow through to implement the change.

During my studies in Positive Psychology led by Harvard Professor Tal Ben-Shahar, PhD, I learned many extremely valuable lessons, and I want to share these with you. One of these lessons is called *Time In*. Ben-Shahar has used it in his lectures as well as in his books *Happier* and *Being Happy*.

Time In is when you stop for a few minutes or more, reflect on the reading, and ask yourself some important questions. The purpose of this procedure is to help you understand the topic you are studying. I highly encourage you to take a moment for *Time In*.

You will also be able to practice the knowledge you gain throughout this book through a number of exercises. You will find these exercises under the sections called *Action*. Please try these activities before moving to the next section of the book so you can begin implementing the lessons you are learning.

In addition to *Time In* and *Action* I have also included substantial findings to support what I teach and practice on a daily basis. Knowing the research behind habits, as well as the research that supports the particular habits I teach in this book, will encourage you to make changes in your life.

This book is divided into three sections.

Part One: What are habits?

You will learn the basics of habits, things that you can do to make habits work for you, recognize different types of habits, and learn how the latest science can help you understand these habits.

Part Two: Committing to new habits

This section of the book will help you make a commitment to develop better habits. You will learn how, why and when your brain changes, get an understanding of the connection between habits and the brain and gain the knowledge and tools to aid you in your journey.

Part Three: How to implement your habits

I will describe practical examples of many habits I have implemented in my own life based on the knowledge that you will learn in Part Two. I don't expect you to implement all or even any of these habits, as they may not interest you but you can use these examples to help define and implement your own habits.

I wish you well on your journey!

"It costs less trouble to fold a paper when it has been folded already. This saving of trouble is due to the essential nature of habit, which brings it about that, to reproduce the effect, a less amount of the outward cause is required."

— From *The Principles of Psychology*
William James, 1890

PART ONE

WHAT ARE HABITS

Successful people are simply those with successful habits.

— Brian Tracy

CHAPTER 1

HABITS AND OUR LIVES

The past to the present

Three years ago, my health was in poor shape. The results of my EKG, which checks for problems with your heart, were not good. I had bad stomachaches every day. Terrible foot pain made it difficult to walk. One of the most well-respected doctors in New York suggested foot surgery to alleviate my pain.

Two months ago at my regular checkup, my doctor told me that my blood pressure was superb, and after checking my lungs he noticed perfect breathing and no alarming sounds. My foot pain had disappeared. He also saw that I'd lost about 30 pounds in three years. "I don't know what you're doing, but whatever it is, keep doing it! You've got amazing results," he said.

I went home and thought about all the changes I made in the past three years. I realized that the improvement of my health is directly linked with my newly acquired habits: by changing my *psychology* I had changed my *physiology*.

What are habits?

Habits are rituals and behaviors that we perform automatically, allowing us to carry out essential activities such as brushing our teeth, taking a shower, getting dressed for work, and following the same routes every day without thinking about them. Our unconscious habits free up resources for our brains to carry out other more complex tasks like solving problems or deciding what to make for dinner.

We all have habits and we activate hundreds every day. These habits can be divided into three groups. The first group are the habits that we simply don't notice because they have been part of our lives forever—like tying shoelaces or brushing teeth. The second are habits that are good for us and which we work hard on establishing—like exercising, eating well or getting enough sleep. The final group are the habits that are bad for us—

like smoking, procrastinating or overspending. But where are all these habits stored?

Scientists have learned that a certain part of the brain called the *basal ganglia* plays a crucial role in creating new habits and maintaining existing ones, leading researchers to an understanding of why some people, even after major brain damage, will still do certain things they've always done before, like find their way home without any conscious previous recollection of where they are going. These people often don't even know how or why they can still do certain things, but if the basal ganglia is intact, those old habits are still available.

The latest research also shows that habits are so ingrained in our brains that we keep acting in accordance with them even when we no longer benefit from them.

Researchers from Duke University have shown that over 40% of what we do is determined not by decisions but by habits. This suggests that we can change a huge part of our lives just by eliminating *bad* habits and creating *good* ones instead. People who fully understand this have been able to find wonderful new ways to change their lives for the better.

The best way to change your bad habits is to directly replace them with new ones. When you create a habit, your brain creates new neurological pathways allowing you to more easily use those habits.

But why do people return to their old habits so often? It's because the neural pathways established as a result of the habits we develop *never get deleted*. Those pathways are always there for us in case we need to go back and use those same routes again. Of course, this helps us in the many simple and automatic daily tasks we carry out such as walking, talking, running, and eating. We don't need to stop and think about how to walk before we get up and do it! (Of course, this applies to the majority of us who are blessed and lucky enough to be able to do so easily).

Since those existing pathways never get erased, the best way to change existing habits is to replace them with new ones.

The Habit Loop

Charles Duhigg, in his book *The Power of Habit* talks about what he calls "The Habit Loop" and explains that every habit is a three step process.

The first step is a *trigger*. A habit starts with a signal; something that triggers your brain to go into automatic mode. The next step is a *routine* (what we do, feel or think). The third and the last step of The Habit Loop is a *reward*.

Your brain decides if the reward is big enough to keep the habit or not. But the problem is that the brain's job is to satisfy a short-term goal.

For example, let's say your goal is to be healthier and lose weight. At lunch time, you find yourself at a place with great hamburgers. If you love hamburgers, your brain will do everything it can to satisfy your immediate desire and make sure you enjoy the hamburger now. It does not focus on your long term goal—to be healthier and lose weight.

This is the beginning of a Habit Loop. If you think carefully about any of the habits you have, you will recognize that there is always some kind of trigger—in this case it is the sight of the burger menu. Your brain then identifies the appropriate habit, and starts an automatic routine. This result is a reward—which in this case is a delicious lunch, even if that may not be what you really need.

To make it clearer, let me explain three habits I have. In the following examples it is important to pay attention to each step of the process (trigger, routine, reward).

Physical habit loop

Every morning I exercise. When I hear my 5 AM alarm, it is a trigger for me to get up, go to my basement and get on the treadmill. The next step in this process is a routine. My routine is to do a 20 minute walk or run. The reward is that I feel really good after exercising—and who wouldn't?

Emotional habit loop

After I finish exercising, I spend some time meditating. The trigger is the end of my run on the treadmill. After that, I sit on the floor, close my eyes, and try to stop thinking and just focus on my breathing. This calms me down and lowers my heart rate after an intense run. It also puts me in a peaceful mood and gives me a clean metal slate on which to work for the rest of the day. That's a reward just by itself.

Thinking habit loop

Not all habits are practiced every day. Some are very occasional, but it doesn't make them any less habitual. The first snow of each winter, for example, triggers a thinking habit that comes to me every year: memories of my childhood in Sarajevo. I spent a lot of time with my friends playing in the snow when I was a boy, and remembering those moments makes me happy. It's just an occasional reward, but it happens every year.

▶▶ 🕐 TIME IN

Think about some of your Habit Loops. What triggers your habits? What are your routines? And finally, what are your rewards?

PRODUCE YOUR OWN HAPPINESS CHEMICAL

Although it is commonly believed that there are 100 billion neurons in the human brain, we still don't know the exact number. Many of the most important chemicals in our body are produced by those neurons. In fact there are chemicals associated with every emotional state we experience. What chemicals would you rather have in your body? The ones that are associated with happiness or the ones that are associated with stress, anger, guilt, etc.? One of the most important chemicals produced by our brain involved in positive habits is dopamine.

Dopamine is the fuel that keeps us motivated. When we achieve a goal, dopamine is released in the brain, making us feel good. Scientists have known for years that dopamine is related to positive behavior, pleasure and joy, but recent studies indicate that dopamine is essential for habit formation.

An even more substantial discovery is that we can tap into our dopamine reserves, and release dopamine at will. This is one of the most important discoveries I have made throughout my research, and I will give you some practical examples of how to apply this knowledge in Part Three of this book.

Releasing more dopamine will help you form positive habits by allowing you to feel joy as a reward. However as discussed earlier, you have to keep in mind your long-term goals while focusing on a short-term craving and desires. Focusing only on your cravings (I love hamburgers, so I will have one) may provide you the immediate pleasure, but may also distract you from establishing your desired habits (a healthy dietary routine).

As humans we are designed to work hard, to feel good when we accomplish something, and to feel bad when we don't. It is wonderful to know that creating a sensation of feeling good is fully within our power.

You should create a sense of reward for yourself every time you achieve something. Even completing the smallest routines such as brushing your teeth, getting dressed, driving to work, opening the door for someone—these are all achievements.

If you see them as more than just a regular routine, you can potentially tap into your dopamine reserve. And when your dopamine is released, you feel good and are ready to achieve your next goal.

To achieve any large goal you need to break it down into small goals. For example, one of my goals was to write this book. But that took some time, and after two years of research, I had still not written a word. It looked like I was getting nowhere.

But my goal wasn't just to write a book. It was also to complete a number of steps along the way. So I broke down my goal into many daily successes.

One of my goals was to write 500 words a day. It was a small aim but by achieving it I increased my dopamine level on a daily basis, and that kept me going until I finished the book.

Now that I understand this process, I know that there was the time when I worked very hard all day and still felt unhappy with the results. At the end of the day I felt I had accomplished nothing, and would go to bed thinking about all the things I had not completed.

I would feel bad, not sleep well and then wake up with a headache…and start all over again. This was a habit of mine that would continue for months and then years. Needless to say, I felt bad about myself, the work I needed to do, and the goals I felt I had not accomplished. Sound familiar?

A friend suggested that at the end of the day, I write down everything that I had done. To my surprise, every time I did this, the list just got longer and longer! Looking back, I now know that by writing down all that I had accomplished I began releasing dopamine into my body.

There are many other ways to produce dopamine, such as to celebrate your successes daily, regardless of how big or small they might be. This celebration could be as simple as telling yourself, "I did it!" By breaking your daily task list into small steps and acknowledging every little step you complete will give you a dopamine boost.

For example, if you decide to wake up at 5 AM to exercise, break this down into small steps. First, wake up. Then get dressed to exercise, get a water bottle ready, run on the treadmill for 20 minutes, take a shower, and get dressed for work. Each of these steps is success in itself.

By being mindful about each step and feeling good about accomplishing each one, dopamine will be released, making you feel joyful!

▶▶🕐 TIME IN

What can I do to produce more dopamine and be happier and closer to reaching my goals, whatever they might be?

UNDERSTAND THAT YOUR BRAIN CHANGES ITSELF

"The brain-matter is plastic", said William James in his book *The Principles of Psychology*, published 1890. It was an incredible discovery.

Science now shows us that the brain is moldable at any stage of life, not only when we are young, but for as long as we live. Research in the area of neuroplasticity shows that changes in behavior can actually cause radical and lasting changes in the makeup of many different parts of your brain.

This remarkable research shows not only that we can change, but that by changing our behavior we are actually putting into process the creation of new neural pathways that radically alter our brains.

Research conducted by Lisa Blackwell of Columbia University and Kali Trzesniewski and

Carol Dweck of Stanford University shows that when students are taught neuroplasticity (how their brain will change as a result of their actions) they perform significantly better in their studies. So just knowing that our brain is plastic will help us produce better results in life. Why is this not common knowledge?

Earlier, I mentioned a study conducted at Duke University which showed that 40% of what we do is determined by habits. Interestingly, research by University of California Professor Sonja Lyubomirsky shows that 40% of our happiness is subject to self-control and behavior (50% is genetic, and only 10% is based on life circumstances).

These are average figures, and individual differences do, of course, play a part. However, the suggestion that behavior plays such a large role in the human experience gives us much to be positive about. We can change 40% or more of our lives just by changing our behavior.

So how does neuroplasticity relate to habits? By changing our habits and behavior, we are, in effect, changing our neural makeup. Forming new habits allows new neural pathways to develop, altering the brain significantly.

Neuroplasticity, although a complicated research area, is a fundamental concept that can be simply explained. The best explanation I have found was put forward by neuroscientist Alvaro Pascual-Leone, who says: "The brain is plastic, not elastic. An elastic band is stretched and always goes back to its original form. The plastic brain is altered by every encounter and every situation. It keeps changing."

A story may explain even more fully. When I was growing up in Sarajevo, there was a hilly street in my neighborhood that would be closed most of the winter to car traffic due to impossible driving conditions. All the kids from the neighborhood, including myself, would go there with sleds—many of them homemade—and climb as high as we possibly could and then sled down.

Sledding from the top of the hill the first time, we would end up at the bottom in a certain place. The second time we went down, we would end up in a different place. The third time we went, we got to yet another place again. As we kept going all day, we would create many different tracks; at the end we began to use certain tracks regularly with almost no effort required on our side.

After sledding down the hill a number of times, we started using well-established paths without even trying. That's exactly what the brain does for us, regardless of whether or not the habits we created are good or bad. The brain will follow the path we have already established.

Now that we know how our brain can change itself, we can look at how we may be able to change our habits accordingly.

▶▶🕐 TIME IN

Think for a moment about the science of neuroplasticity and how your brain is constantly changing. Visualize your brain as playdough that you can shape using your willpower. On which tracks are you riding your life? Do you need to introduce new tracks? Think about the new kinds of tracks that you may want to develop, and some that you may want to change.

FROM DESTRUCTIVE TO CONSTRUCTIVE

When Charles Duhigg went to Iraq in 2003 as a news reporter he noticed something very curious. The town of Kufa was extremely violent, until one day it suddenly was not. No one knew why, but there was something going on in the background that could explain it.

Charles went to see the army major in charge of the unit controlling this part of Iraq, and found that he was conducting a "Habit Modification Program."

The major had been analyzing videos of violence day after day, and he noticed patterns: a crowd would gather, more and more people would show up, someone would throw a rock, the crowd would start chanting, and the violence would begin.

He also noticed something else of interest. Late in the afternoon, food vendors would show up and everyone would eat, and shortly thereafter violence would break out. In light of these findings, he went to the mayor of Kufa and made a rather unusual request. He asked if the mayor would keep food vendors outside of the area, and the mayor agreed to this.

The next day the crowd came as usual, and ultimately get tired and hungry. They awaited their usual food vendors to buy kebab, but they weren't there. Slowly, a new habit developed among the crowd. The crowd would disperse and people would go home. Within two weeks, the unrest in Kufa stopped.

The army major identified one small habit among a group of people, and ultimately stopped their violent behavior.

▶▶🕐 TIME IN

Can you think of one habit of yours that is destructive to you? What is it? Can you now identify the elements that can possibly help you turn that *destructive* habit into a *constructive* habit?

Rigid, the skeleton of habit alone upholds the human frame.

—Virginia Woolf

CHAPTER 2

ELEMENTS OF HABITS

It is important not just to identify what your habits are, but to be aware of and understand each element of them.

Merriam Webster defines habits as:

a. *Behavioral patterns acquired through frequent repetition or physiological exposure that shows itself in regularity or increased facility of performance.*

b. *acquired modes of behavior that have become nearly or completely involuntary.*

Since many habits fall into the definition of "behaviors that have become nearly or completely involuntary", you first need to believe that you can change them. Once you overcome that step you can work on fully understanding your habits, analyzing them, and ultimately changing them as necessary.

Our habits are related to a number of situations, and you need to be able to recognize them: the time of day when the activity begins, where it happens, who you are with, your emotional state, and what you do immediately after the habit. By addressing some of these elements you will make significant steps towards changing any existing negative habits and developing positive new ones.

Making a chart may help. Here is mine:

Habit	Day/Time	Location	Other People	Emotional State	Immediately After
Wake up with a smile	Mon – Fri 5am	My House	My wife next to me	Happy	Get up with a smile
Exercise	Mon – Fri 5.05am	My Basement	None	Energized	Meditate
Meditation	Mon – Fri 5.35am	My Basement	None	Calm	Take a shower
An Attitude for Gratitude	Mon – Fri About 5.50am	Shower	None	Grateful	Get ready to go to work
Walking	Mon – Fri About 7pm	Home Neighborhood	My wife	Benevolence	Read

▶▶⊕ TIME IN

Think for a moment about your habits. What habits do you have? Focus on one particular habit. At what time do you do this? Where? Who is with you? What emotions do you have? What do you do immediately after you complete this habit?

⟳ ACTION

On the following page, identify, document and analyze your habits. This action will help you get a deeper understanding of your good habits and help you change your bad ones.

Habit	Day/Time	Location	Other People	Emotional State	Immediately After

PAY CLOSE ATTENTION TO YOUR EXISTING HABITS

Before you start changing your habits, you need to understand your existing ones. The following are sample questions you can ask yourself in order to understand your existing habits.

- What is the first thing I do when I hear the alarm clock? (Snooze? Stay in bed for five minutes longer? Get up immediately? Get upset and angry because I have to get up? Smile? Kiss my partner?)
- What is the next thing I do? (Take a shower? Eat breakfast? Get ready to exercise? Meditate? Turn on the TV?)
- What do I do then? (Get into the car and drive to work? Study? Check email?)
- What other habits do I have throughout

the day? (What else do I do when drinking coffee, having a snack, going out for lunch, socializing with my coworkers, browsing the internet?)

- What do I do in the evening before I go to sleep? (Watch TV? Browse the internet? Exercise? Read? Go out for a walk?)

Gerry, a friend of mine, did this exercise. With his permission, I will share part of what he did.

Question: When do I eat snacks?

Answer: I have cookie after lunch.

Question: When do I drink soda?

Answer: With lunch and dinner.

Question: What do I do after dinner?

Answer: Browse the internet and check Facebook.

Question: What do I do immediately after?

Answer: Watch TV.

Question: What do I do while watching TV?

Answer: Eat peanuts.

▶▶🕐 TIME IN

Think about your day from the time when you wake up to when you go to sleep. What habits do you have? What do you do first thing in the morning? What do you eat for breakfast? What time do you leave home for work?

If you work from home, what does your day look like?

What do you do before dinner? What do you do immediately after dinner?

💲ACTION

Write down questions you can ask yourself to help you understand your existing habits. Answer the questions.

Question: _____

Answer: _____

Question: _____

Answer: _____

Question: _____

Answer: _____

When Gerry did the above exercise, it helped him create a list of his existing habits and also decide whether or not to keep those habits. Here is short list of what he had.

My Existing Habits	Keep it	
	YES	NO
Eat healthy breakfast	YES	
Exercise five days a week	YES	
Drink soda		NO
Eat peanuts after dinner		NO
Eat cookies every day		NO
Meditate five minutes a day	YES	
Spend too much time watching TV		NO

⇔ ACTION

On the following page, write down as many of your habits as you can. Next to each habit identify whether you want to keep it (YES) or not (NO).

My Existing Habits	Keep it	
	YES	NO

HOW ONE HABIT CAN TRIGGER ANOTHER

Before you make a move towards developing new habits, you also need to take into acccount how one habit can trigger another. This technique will help you introduce multiple routines into many areas of your life effectively.

For example, I exercise at 5 AM every morning, and at the end of my exercise routine I meditate. So the trigger for my meditation is the end of my exercise. Immediately following my meditation routine, I do a breathing exercise (a breathing exercise is also considered a mediation practice). The trigger for my breathing exercise is the end of my meditation.

So I introduced three habits into one sequence. This ensures that I actually succeed in practicing all three habits every day, at the exact same time and within that same environment.

▶▶🕐 TIME IN

Think of a habit you have that triggers another habit. How can you use such a process to your advantage? What sort of triggers can you create to introduce new habits?

WHEN A TRIGGER IS MISSING

Knowing exactly what triggers a habit is a major key to success because the trigger is as important as defining the habit itself. Let me explain.

Every morning I carry out my *Gratitude* habit. In this routine I express my gratitude out loud for people and things in my life. I perform this habit in the shower so it goes perfectly with another automatic habit (taking a shower).

My bathroom is painted yellow. The color is a trigger for my gratitude habit. When I am home, I perform this habit every day.

When I went on vacation, I realized I hadn't done my gratitude exercise for a few days. I saw that the hotel bathroom did not have the same yellow wall as I have in my house. Therefore the trigger for this habit was missing. That was the reason I was skipping my routine.

I realized that my trigger was too specific, so I decided to make it more generic. Now, as soon as I turn the shower on I start my habit. Ever since introducing this generic trigger, I have not missed a day of my gratitude habit.

⟡ ACTION

Find a generic trigger for any new routine you try to develop. That will set your habit in motion regardless of the external environment.

IMPROVING YOUR WILLPOWER

If you can improve your willpower, you will be much more able to make the sort of positive changes you want to see. There are many tools at your disposal with which you can improve your willpower.

In his course, *The Neuroscience of Everyday Life*, Professor Sam Wang explains willpower from the perspective of a neuroscientist. He understands that willpower is just like a muscle. With exercise, it gets stronger.

What would happen if you didn't regularly exercise and then, without any preparation, you attempted a marathon? There is a strong chance you wouldn't be able to finish. In fact, you could even do more harm to your body than good. The same thing applies to our willpower. To get stronger and improve our overall self-control, we need to practice and develop it incrementally. But if we try to over-extend our willpower—just like the under-prepared marathon runner—we run the risk of failing, not just once, but over and over again.

To understand willpower and self control, let's look at a famous experiment conducted in 1996 by the psychologist Roy Baumeister.

Baumeister asked a group of people not to eat anything three hours prior to coming to the laboratory. Most of the participants came in hungry and ready to eat. The scientists prepared freshly baked chocolate cookies and placed them throughout the room so the entire place smelled strongly of the cookies.

The participants were divided into three groups. One group was asked to eat the cookies. Another group was asked to eat radishes placed in the same room. The third group was in the same room but was offered no food at all.

The participants who were directed to eat radishes and not to eat cookies struggled with temptation (some even picked up the cookies and smelled them), but no one from this group ate them.

Then all the participants were taken into another room. The researchers gave them a puzzle—one that was impossible to solve. But the participants were not aware of that.

Those who were directed to eat the cookies worked on the problem for about 20 minutes. So did the group that was offered no food. The participants who were told to eat radishes and had to resist cookies gave up after an average of eight minutes.

The researchers agreed that the same energy is required to resist something (in this case the cookies) as it is to work on the puzzle. The group that ate radishes but had to resist cookies depleted their energy (willpower) while resisting what they desired. So they had very little willpower left while trying to solve the problem. The other two groups had enough self control to work on the problem much longer.

This shows that our willpower is limited, and that we have to carefully choose when and how to use it, just like a muscle. In other words, if you happen to have an important meeting, a test to take, or a presentation to give, do not try to exercise your self control by rejecting simple desires like chocolate immediately prior to that meeting.

If you do, your willpower may become depleted, which may affect the outcome of your task. You need to carefully choose when to exercise your self-control and when not to.

The bad news is, if you try to over-extend your self-control you can lose motivation for other important activities in your life. The good news is that you can extend your willpower just like you can extend your muscles.

You can start increasing your willpower straight away by taking baby steps in changing certain small habits. One way to improve your willpower is to keep attempting to do things you've never done before. For example, for one week try one of the following: pick up utensils or use the computer mouse with your non-dominant hand. Take the stairs instead of the elevator. Eat food you have never eaten before. Get the idea?

Tom Rath a Senior scientist at Gallup shows that in another study of habits, people who ate with their non-dominant hands ate less (in this particular study they were eating popcorn). So in addition to improving your willpower, chances are you will also eat less. You gain two huge benefits of introducing one habit. Not bad!

Another interesting piece of research done at Case Western Reserve University showed that making small changes in your habits such as brushing your teeth with your non-dominant hand can improve your willpower.

I've brushed my teeth with my dominant hand throughout my entire life, and never had a second thought about it. It was a habit I'd established, and I wasn't about to break it. However, after learning about this research I decided to give it a shot.

To enhance the effectiveness of the change process, I placed my toothbrush and toothpaste on my left side in order to remind myself to pick it up with my left hand.

At first, this did not make much of a difference, but after a week or so I got into the habit of picking up my toothbrush with my left hand. Every once in a while my right hand would automatically attempt to grab the toothbrush, but I would become conscious of this before brushing and switch hands.

Your net worth to the world is usually determined by what remains after your bad habits are subtracted from your good ones.

—Benjamin Franklin

CHAPTER 3

TYPES OF HABITS

When we think of habits, we usually think of something that we do (driving, running, brushing our teeth). These are physical habits. There are also emotional and thinking habits. To that list, I will add what I call *circle habits*.

Before you make a commitment to change your existing habits and implement new ones, let's go over each type in little more detail.

Physical habits

Thanks to a very complicated and intelligent brain mechanism, we all have a number of physical habits. Most of them we never even think about, such as driving a car. Once we've learned how to drive, we never forget how to, and the more we drive the better we become. We listen to music, talk to our passengers, all while paying attention to the road, street signs, and other cars. We perform many actions, some involuntarily, all simultaneously—and many become habits.

Another example of a physical habit is exercise. Once exercise becomes a habit it can also enter into autopilot mode. Your *unconscious brain* will also try to activate such routines even when your *conscious brain* is not thinking about it.

Emotional habits

There are many *emotional habits* that we don't necessarily think of as habits. We just think of them as emotions and nothing more. However, habits are influenced greatly by our emotional state. Being happy, sad, angry or upset could all be routines that you create unknowingly.

Just like any other habits, there are emotional states that serve us well and others that don't. Feeling happy while spending time with your closest family members, being excited for the success of your partner, friends or children, feeling gratefulness for the life you have, etc.— these habits serve us well.

We also have emotional habits such as anger, envy, sadness, jealousy, etc. which are not as good for us. The key is to identify these habits in specific situations and see what we can do to change them.

Every night, I read between 8 PM and 9 PM. This is a plan I have created (in place of watching television) that serves me well. Recently, however, I was puzzled as to why I sometimes became agitated, distracted and unable to sleep, and why my reaction to normal communication with my wife changed.

One night, after thinking about my change in mood (usually between the hours 8 PM and 9 PM), I realized my disharmony occurred only after unexpected circumstances needed my attention, and therefore my reading time was compromised or missed altogether.

An hour of reading is enjoyable. So naturally, only reading for 15 minutes is less so. Having no reading time at all triggered a negative change of mood and was leading me to become angry. Thankfully I've developed an understanding and awareness of this, and have subsequently changed my habitual behavior.

As soon as I notice that my reading time will be compromised or missed, I concisely focus on the benefits and importance of the task I am working on instead. That focus gives me a satisfaction of completing an important task rather than anger for not reading.

Now that I'm aware of the relationship between my habits and emotional state, I can watch and manage each accordingly. I tell myself these emotions are normal, yet such negative emotions and anger can make me feel unwell, and it's also not fair to my wife. She doesn't deserve to deal with my negative mood, and the only reason I get upset is because I've created a habit of getting upset in this situation.

I now know why my negative mood is sometimes triggered during my scheduled reading time. I reason with myself by understanding that these interruptions are rare and that most of the time I do get at least one hour of scheduled reading. I also take the time to be grateful that I am able to complete an unexpected but important task even though it may have interrupted my scheduled reading time.

▶▶⏱ TIME IN

Think for a moment about the emotional habits you may have. Think of a time you've been happy, sad, or upset. What triggered it? What goes through your mind during such times? What do you usually feel and do? What would you rather do?

Thinking habits

Thinking habits are extremely important, as everything that you do consciously starts with a thought. Your thinking defines not only your emotions but also your actions, and of course your emotions drive your actions too.

If you think and believe that you can do something, and find a great reason to do it, you will find a way.

We see many people who are happy and enthusiastic in the morning, and we also see many people who are miserable. It's up to you to decide which category you want to be in. You are the only one who can make that choice.

You need to be thinking about your thinking. This is known as *meta cognition* and going through this process can help you greatly.

I have a friend named Greg. Greg used to get very depressed, but he learned to start thinking about what caused his depression and, more importantly, the behavior that follows.

He realized that by breaking thought with action, he could make a huge difference. Any time he started to get depressed, he would run on the treadmill or do some other kind of physical activity. That would cut the established thinking habit out and allow for the creation of a new habit.

Once he followed that routine regularly, he went into positive autopilot to steer clear of any negative thoughts. In *thinking about his thinking*, he was able to change his habits through his behavior.

However, thinking alone will not make a difference. Greg acted on his thoughts and broke his bad thinking habit.

We all have our fair share of negative thoughts. The question isn't whether you have them, but what you do with them and how you act as a result.

Remain aware of negative thoughts, and watch your behavior during and shortly after having such thoughts. Once you start noticing and becoming aware of your negative thought patterns, you can set about changing your thoughts, and subsequently alter your behavior. Eventually this process will become easier, and you will be able to minimize your negative thoughts.

▶▶ 🕐 TIME IN

What goes through your mind when you feel that you have failed to achieve one of your goals? How about when you succeed? Do you trust that you can do anything if you put your mind to it? Why? Why not?

Circle habits

We've all made promises to ourselves to change bad old habits and introduce good new ones. Maybe you've wanted to quit smoking or begin exercising. Maybe you've wanted to spend less time in the office and more time with your family. Whatever the case may be, it's not always difficult to start. Going one day without a cigarette, or spending 20 minutes on a single day exercising is the easy part. The difficulty is finding a way to keep going amid adversity.

An easy way to explain this is to tell a personal story. About ten years ago, I was lucky enough to work for a company that had a fitness center on the premises. It was a great opportunity. For months, I went to the gym five days a week. I felt great and thought: nothing can stop me now.

But change is inevitable. Five years ago, I accepted an excellent leadership position with another company. The rewarding new job was also demanding. It was often essential that I get to the office early and stay late. On top of that, this new job was further from my home. I sometimes spent four hours getting to and from work on days with bad traffic.

For two years, I kept telling myself that I would get back to my exercise routine. And the longer I kept saying I would do it without actually doing it, the more frustrated I became. It drove me crazy. I finally realized I had two options: either begin exercising, or put the idea out of my head and reevaluate at a later point. I decided on the latter, and told myself to come back to it in six weeks time.

By doing that, I closed one of my Circle Habits. Circle Habits are promises we make to ourselves but cannot keep. They are broken habits. They are ideas we want to put in place, but, for whatever reason, have difficulty sustaining. They are circular because we keep coming back to them at the beginning. We run them through our heads repeatedly, as if on a closed circuit, but cannot actually get them into place. Or, if we can get them into place, we have a hard time sustaining them. In my case, thinking about exercise had become my habit, instead of actual exercise.

The point is that you don't have to close a Circle Habit by beginning a new routine immediately. It's perfectly acceptable to close it by putting the idea for your new habit away for a while. If you cannot find time to exercise today, don't torture yourself over it. Set it aside for a set period of time—a week, maybe, or a month—and come back to it later. That is one way to close a habit loop.

This isn't an absolute solution. It would be easy to say you have no time to work on any habits, and to always put them aside for later. So be careful to only bracket ideas that you really cannot prioritize. Don't put off improving your habits unless you will come back to them at a fixed point.

It worked for me. Six weeks after making a promise to myself to reevaluate my exercise routine, I found that I was comfortable enough at my new job to afford myself some additional time at the gym. By then, I had begun exercising a few days a week again, which was just the amount of time I needed.

▶▶ 🕐 TIME IN

Identify a habit you want to put into place. What's holding you back? Is it something you can work around today? If not, bracket the idea for later. Close the Circle Habit by coming back to it when you have more time or energy. Put it out of your mind entirely and don't let it get you down. In the meantime, do what you can to improve other habits. But don't forget to come back to your old idea.

The more of the details of our daily life we can hand over to the effortless custody of automatism, the more our higher powers of mind will be set free for their own proper work ... If there be such daily duties not yet ingrained in any one of my readers, let him begin this very hour to set the matter right.

– From *The Principles of Psychology*
William James, 1890

PART TWO

COMMITING TO
NEW HABITS

Your beliefs become your thoughts,
Your thoughts become your words,
Your words become your actions,
Your actions become your habits,
Your habits become your values,
Your values become your destiny.

– Mahatma Gandhi

CHAPTER 4

DEVELOPING BETTER HABITS

Believe you can change your habits

I was not convinced that beliefs had a huge impact on habits until I read *The Biology of Belief* by Bruce Lipton. Lipton is a former medical school Professor and research scientist who examined the mechanism by which cells receive and process information, and after years of research he found that biology adapts to our beliefs.

According to his research, our beliefs control our behavior—and can even control our genes. By changing our behavior, we can change our habits and consequently our lives.

If you believe—*truly believe*—you can change your old habits or introduce new ones, that belief will control your behavior. Because of that I would recommend that you primarily work on those habits that you believe you can change or introduce into your life.

For example, let's say I want to establish a habit of daily exercise. First of all, I very much believe and know that I can establish this habit. I also believe that I will find the time to do it. If need be, I will stop doing something else that is less important to me at this point. If nothing works, I believe I can wake up 20 minutes earlier than usual to establish this habit. I strongly believe (and this is actually a fact) that this habit will help me improve my overall wellbeing. Therefore, my belief will drive my behavior toward achieving this habit and putting it in place.

▶▶ 🕐 TIME IN

Which of your habits do you believe you can change? Why? Which new habit can you introduce into your life? Why? Do you *really* believe you can do this?

List those habits and make a commitment.

FIND YOUR MOTIVATION

Another thing you need to keep in mind, and something that we will cover in more detail, is motivation. You need to be highly motivated for the establishment of new habits to work effectively.

By this, I mean that you must have a strong reason for establishing your new habit. This becomes your motivation, and needs to be something that resonates with you personally, and not just something that someone else wants you to do.

Friedrich Nietzsche once said, "He who has a 'Why' to live for can bear almost any 'How.'" Therefore, in order to change and/or introduce a new habit, you must have a strong *why*, otherwise the change will not happen. A strong *why* will motivate you and help you make the necessary shift.

▶▶ ⏱ TIME IN

Think for a moment about one habit you want to change or a new one you want to introduce into your life. How motivated are you to introduce this habit? Why do you want to do it? Do you have a *why* strong enough to make it happen?

Just Keep Starting

In his book, *The Now Habit at Work*, Neil Fiore introduces the idea of "Just Keep Starting." Starting the process of creating new habits is difficult, especially if the idea for a new habit is a routine that may take, say, 30 minutes a day, three or four days a week (or more). If on top of that you are struggling with motivation, it will not be easy to implement that habit.

Instead of thinking about how something might be impossible to achieve, think about *just starting*. Even start by exercising five minutes a day. We can all find five minutes in our day. It's hard to find an excuse to not "just start" with such a routine.

If you're really struggling for the motivation to get up and "just start", how about developing some sort of progressive schedule like this:

Day 1: Put your sneakers on and keep them on for five minutes
Day 2: Take a steady walk for five minutes
Day 3: Take a steady walk for six minutes
Day 4: Take a steady walk for seven minutes

Keep developing a similar plan until you reach the point where you want to be with this habit (i.e. walk for 20 minutes). By doing this you are building strong new habits.

It is more than adequate to spend five minutes a day on any new habit that you want to develop, for as many days as it takes you to get into your routine. Just five minutes a day will go a long way towards solidifying that habit in a short time if you put in the necessary work.

▶▶🕐 TIME IN

Think about a habit that you've wanted to implement but that you just couldn't find the time to develop it. Can you "Just Keep Starting"?

ACTIVATION ENERGY

To start any new habit, you will need what psychologist Mihaly Csikszentmihalyi calls the "activation energy"—the initial energy required to get you started. Nothing happens without the initial spark.

But how long does it take to create that initial spark? Days? Hours? Minutes? It certainly depends of what you are trying to accomplish as well as your own personality. Some of us will keep pushing until we get what we want, while others take their time.

One rule, the "20-Second Rule," is a positive psychology principle introduced by Shawn Achor. Achor wanted to begin playing guitar but three weeks after committing to his habit, he realized he had only played four times.

Realizing something was amiss, Shawn took his guitar from the closet and placed it in the middle of his room. Three weeks later, he noticed he hadn't missed a single day of playing. By conveniently putting his guitar in plain sight, he *decreased* the "activation energy" required to start his new habit.

What was different? The guitar was right in front of him, and not tucked inside his closet, 20 seconds away. Now that he learned how his brain worked, Shawn knew he could trick his brain the same way his brain had tricked him.

He applied the same idea when he decided to cut down on the time he spent watching TV. In order for this new habit to be implemented, he removed the batteries from his remote control and placed them 20 seconds away in a drawer in his bedroom. He now had to *increase* the activation energy that would take him to go to his bedroom and pick up the batteries.

To *introduce* a new habit, we need to *decrease* the activation energy for 20 seconds (make it as convenient as possible to start a new habit), and to *avoid* an existing habit, we need to *increase* the activation energy for 20 seconds (make it inconvenient to continue the existing habit).

▶▶🕐 TIME IN

Where can you apply the 20-Second Rule?

Think of a habit you want to implement. What do you need to do to decrease the activation energy?

Now think of a habit you have but want to stop. What can you do to increase the activation energy?

MAKE AN ANNOUNCEMENT

William James referenced Scottish philosopher Alexander Bain when he said "In the acquisition of a new habit, or the leaving off of an old one, we must ... take a public pledge." I'm a firm believer in *announcing* habits.

When I began my new exercise routine I told many friends what my plan was: to get up at 5 AM, and exercise. The more people I told, the more I felt committed to continue my habit. After all, how could I disappoint my friends and myself?

So go ahead: tell everyone about your new habits. Commit to them and make yourself accountable.

▶▶ ⏱ TIME IN

Have you made an announcement today about a new habit of yours? How big was the announcement for you? How many people know about it? Go and tell everyone! Call your friends, family members and colleagues. Send them an email. Publish it on Facebook. Tweet it. The more announcements, the better.

ACCOUNTABILITY PARTNER

Research shows that people who have an exercise partner have a better chance of successfully losing weight; but this can be applied to any habit you are trying to implement.

Based on this, I suggest you find an accountability partner. An accountability partner is someone who has already successfully implemented a habit you want to work on, or who is highly motivated and dedicated to implement that same habit (i.e. going to the gym together, helping each other choose the right food, losing weight, studying new subjects, etc.).

↻ ACTION

List all the habits you want to work on and write down the name of a potential accountability partner next to each habit.

Habit	Accountability partner
1.	
2.	
3.	
4.	
5.	
6.	
7.	
8.	
9.	
10.	

SUPPORT GROUP

Today, there are many support groups to help people manage and overcome issues such as addiction, grief, eating disorders, anxiety, etc.

To establish certain habits, in addition to having an accountability partner, a support group may be useful. A study of weight loss groups with 10,000 participants, published in the British Medical Journal, shows that those in a support group lost 15.2 more pounds on average than those with no support group.

Now that we have this knowledge, let's apply it to any habit we want to implement. It does not need to be a large nor an official support group. Signing up a few friends to work on a common goal will help you and your friends implement a new habit regardless of what the habit is.

▶▶🕐 TIME IN

Would it help if you had an accountability partner? How about a support group? Who can be your accountability partner or a member of your support group?

REWARD YOURSELF

Many people, from self-help gurus to researchers at the National Institute for Health, will tell you to celebrate your achievements, and to set rewards to stay motivated

Come up with your own way of rewarding yourself with whatever works for you. This could be buying some new running gear, a movie theater visit, a new book, or a visit to your favorite restaurant.

You need to watch out for things that you consider rewards, but which could actually be counterproductive and slow you down in your efforts to establish positive new habits, like skipping a day of working out and eating fatty foods when your goal is to establish new workout routines or to lose weight.

▶▶🕐 TIME IN

Which habit did you start working on? Did you reward yourself for the work you did? If not, think of a reward. Go ahead! You deserve it.

"Accumulate all the possible circumstances which shall reinforce the right motives; put yourself assiduously in conditions that encourage the new way; make engagements incompatible with the old; take a public pledge, if the case allows; in short, envelop your resolution with every aid you know.

This will give your new beginning such a momentum that the temptation to break down will not occur as soon as it otherwise might; and every day during which a breakdown is postponed adds to the chances of its not occurring at all."

– From *The Principles of Psychology*
William James, 1890

PART THREE

HOW TO
IMPLEMENT
YOUR HABITS

**Men's natures are alike;
it is their habits that separate them.**

– Confucius

CHAPTER 5

OUT WITH THE OLD, IN WITH THE NEW

By now I hope you are committed to making habitual changes in your life, and have decided it's time to replace some old habits with new ones. To help you do this I will give personal examples, recommend specific actions to take, and provide some practical exercises. Please keep in mind that the information on the following pages can be applied to other habits you may want to introduce in your life.

THE SMALL WINS HABIT

Many of the habits I talk about in this book require a lot of persistence. But that's nothing new. What is new is that there is a habit that you can implement that can help you become persistent and make it easier for you to implement your other habits.

You may recall from Part One of this book that when we achieve a goal, our body releases a chemical call dopamine. Why is that important? Because dopamine is a happy chemical that makes us feel good and it is a human nature that when we feel good, we want to continue feeling good.

This means that even if we finish a small but measurable portion of our goals, our bodies will release some dopamine. So to get started, instead of focusing on a big goal, a habit that takes lot of effort and willpower to implement, I suggest focus on a small goal, a small habit, or a small portion of a habit.

Karl Weick from the University of Texas in his book *Redefining the Scale of Social Issues*, defines what he calls "Small Wins." These small wins help us accomplish our big tasks. Small wins will make you think that it's not a big deal to complete a task and it will make it easier to do.

When you began committing to new habits (in Part Two) you learned about the process Neil Fiore calls "Just Keep Starting." You may recall that I gave you an example of developing an exercise habit in which you commit for only five minutes a day until you get ready to exercise longer. This is a Small Wins Habit.

For example in my home office, I have many old technology books that need to be thrown away to make space for new books. This is a huge task and I keep dreading it.

But if I apply small wins, I create a new habit. So now, every time I leave my office, I take a few books with me to throw out. My office has already started looking much better.

▶▶ ⏱ TIME IN

What big task do you want to take on? Think about breaking it down into small, manageable parts.

✧ ACTION

Identify a habit where you want to apply the Small Wins Approach. Outline small steps toward implementing your habit (for example if your goal is to exercise 45 minutes, start exercising 5 minutes every day). Outline the first small step. Do it. Outline the next small step. Do it. Just do it!

THE EXERCISE HABIT

"I don't have time for exercise" is what we keep telling ourselves and others, and our mind begins to agree. Our brain says "if you don't have any time for it, I'm not going to put any effort into it." How do you convince yourself to do otherwise?

Once again, you need to find the *why* in wanting to exercise. The reason needs to be strong enough to conquer any potential rationale against developing this new routine. For example, wanting to live longer, to have more energy, or to be healthier are all good *whys*.

Frank Hu, Associate Professor of nutrition and epidemiology at the Harvard School of Public Health, says that the single thing that comes close to a magic bullet, in terms of its universal benefits, is exercise. Exercise can prevent heart disease, strokes, diabetes and many kinds of cancer. It will improve your brain, blood flow and bone density. Enough good reasons?

To implement a new exercise habit, the first thing you must do is schedule a time at which you want to execute this new habit. Just telling yourself that you will exercise three, four, or five days a week without scheduling specific times will simply not help you establish a routine. Therefore you need to pick definite and specific times and days. When I introduced the exercise habit I decided that I would exercise every day at 5 AM for 20 minutes.

Before I established my exercise routine, I struggled. I had tried to develop similar routines a number of times before, but somehow my motivation always died. I would start my exercise routine, and would still always find a reason to stop—like starting a new job and not having the time, having to leave too early in the morning for work, coming back from work late and tired, etc.

You must be motivated in order to achieve anything substantial. Most of the time you need *positive motivation.* You need to understand all of the positive things that will come out of developing your new habit. However, when that does not work you may need another form of motivation, *negative motivation*: "What will happen if I don't do this?"

In the past I didn't have strong enough positive or negative motivation to push me into continuing my regular exercise. But given that both of my parents died young, one day it hit me. What if the same happens to me? What if my son loses his father at a young age like I did?

Do I want my wife to struggle and be without her best friend? Don't my future grandchildren deserve a chance to play with their grandfather? How about my friends? Why should they lose me?

After answering these questions, I realized it was my responsibility to be here on this beautiful planet for as long as possible. Suddenly, that was enough motivation for me to get serious about planning my exercise routine.

To start a habit of physical exercise, the first thing to do is to set precise routines broken down into smaller tasks. This could include preparing running clothes the night before your exercise routine or leaving shoes next to your bed so they will be the first thing you see when you wake up. Shawn Achor went as far as sleeping in his gym clothes, so as soon as he woke up, he was ready to go to gym.

It is hard to find a reason against exercising for only five minutes a day. You may think five minutes is too short an exertion to even be worthwhile, but the amount of time should be limited in the beginning. You need to be absolutely certain of maintaining your motivation levels. As you continue with the exercise habit on a daily basis, you can keep increasing the duration until your desired time is reached.

Once you've exercised for about 30 days in a row your habit should become firmly established. By this time you should look forward to exercising and fulfilling your daily routine. If for some reason you can't fulfill your exercise routine on a particular day, your brain might even begin to miss it. This is the sort of state of mind you're ultimately seeking to develop.

▶▶ ⏱ TIME IN

What kind of physical activity do you do in an average day? Is it enough to keep you healthy and happy? Do you need to do more? If so, now is the time to make that commitment.

⟳ ACTION

Commit to some form of exercise. Write down your Exercise Schedule and stick to it. Start small. Five minutes a day is a great start until your brain gets used to it and starts liking it. Keep doing it until becomes a habit.

THE MEASURING EXERCISE SUCCESS HABIT

There is a reason fancy gym equipment has digital readouts that tell you how many calories you've burned, how long you've been exercising, your heart rate, etc. Our brains love to see these measurements. Measurements are marks of our success or failure. When we do well, these readouts are our reward, but when we don't, they are an indicator that we need to do better.

A substantial body of research published in the Surgeon General's 2008 annual report recommends that adults walk at least 10,000 steps a day. This level of physical activity can be met by plenty of everyday walking, running, swimming, dancing, etc.

Martin Seligman, who pioneered the field of Positive Psychology, measures his success with a pedometer. He started a group with some friends who report to one another each day on how many steps they have taken.

Seligman says that if he hasn't walked 10,000 steps by the end of the day, he will go out for a walk around the house until he reaches that minimum. This is an ingenious way to keep up with your exercise routine and a great idea of a new habit you could develop.

▶▶⏲ TIME IN

How do you know you have done enough exercise in your day? How do you measure the success of your physical activity?

⇕ ACTION

Find a definitive way that works for you to measure progress of your exercise. Keep a daily log in your journal, computer, on your phone, or any other form of log that you deem appropriate.

THE MEASURING WEIGH HABIT

Regardless of whether you want to lose weight, gain weight or simply stay with your current weight, one of the most efficient ways of doing so is to measure your progress on a daily basis. This is an easy habit to implement, and it will tell you a great story about your daily routines. By having this habit, you will know every day if you had too much, too little, or just the right amount of good food and exercise.

You can do this by creating a log. I started with one that looked like this:

Date: i.e. 1/1/2013
Weight: x pounds

I ask my wife to join me in this effort. I relied on the *Accountability Partner* research knowing that we will both benefit from doing this together.

The new form now looked like this:

Date:	i.e. 1/1/2013
Braco (Weight):	x pounds
Nevenka (Weight):	x pounds

At the end of the month, the person who lost the higher weight percentage would get a reward that we identified in advance.

Two years later, we still get on the scales every morning. It is an extremely useful and important habit that helps us manage our lives and get immediate measurable feedback.

This routine will dramatically help you change other habits that in turn will help you lose, gain or stay on the same weight level, and more importantly, be healthier.

▶▶ ⏰ TIME IN

How often do you weigh yourself? If not very often, how do you know you stay on track? What is your ideal weight?

⟳ ACTION

Create a habit of getting on the scale every day at the same time.

THE FIVE DEEP BREATHS HABIT

"Take a deep breath" is commonly taken as a figure of speech, but many people don't understand what deep breathing can actually do for us physically and mentally.

Throughout history, many teachers have believed that deliberate breathing exercises can be extremely valuable in enhancing our wellbeing. Numerous studies have now given us solid evidence of the positive effects that breathing exercises can have on the nervous system.

One such study by Richard P. Brown and Patricia L. Gerb published in *Annals of the New York Academy of Sciences* showed that breathing exercises can rapidly bring us to the present moment and reduce stress.

In addition, this research shows that breathing exercises can improve your heart rate, and help treat depression, anxiety and post-traumatic stress disorder.

Utilizing breathing techniques and drawing on work by martial arts expert Thomas Crum, I use the following exercise multiple times every day, the first being right after my meditation routine, called "Three Deep Breaths."

I have extended Crum's three breaths to five breaths. Keep in mind that this is a flexible exercise and you should create one that works for you.

The following are detailed directions for this exercise:

First breath

Take a deep breath and breathe out.

Second breath

Inhale again and as you exhale, express your gratitude. For example:
- I am grateful for my health.
- I am grateful for my children.
- I am grateful for my wife.

Third breath

Take another breath in and exhale. Focus on one thing that *you want to be* today. For example:

- Today I will be calm.
- Today I will be patient.
- Today I will let go of judgment.

Fourth breath

Inhale again and as you exhale say aloud a thought that represents your ideal self. Who are you or who do you want to be? For example:

- I am a loving, generous individual who always strives to do the right thing.
- I am a kind human being who wants to help others.
- I am a mindful individual and I live in the moment as much as possible.

Fifth breath

Take a deep breath in and out to finish.

▶▶⏱ TIME IN

Take a deep breath. Take two more. Take five deep breaths. How does it feel? Make a commitment to do this at least once a day.

⟳ ACTION

Create your own Five Deep Breath Exercise based on the sequence presented here. Write it on a piece of paper or on the computer and print it out. Place it somewhere in your house where you can see it so it can also serve as a reminder for you do perform it often.

THE GRATITUDE HABIT

Although your parents may often have told you to "count your blessings and not your troubles", it may not have been obvious why this was so important.

Since learning about habits I have seen substantial evidence to support the idea that if we take some time to appreciate the life we have, we can improve our wellbeing significantly.

In financial terms, when something appreciates, it increases in value. When our financial stock appreciates, it is worth more than what we originally paid. When we appreciate other people, and life around us, we recognize more good things in life and increase the value of these good things. Dr. Tal Ben-Shahar says it the best: "When we appreciate the good, the good appreciates."

Once I realized the importance of gratitude, I developed my own Gratitude habit, which has become a routine I follow every morning. This is a time when I express my gratitude for the many positive things in my life.

I have an interesting trigger for this habit (which you may remember from Chapter 2)—the shower. Every time I turn on the shower my gratitude habit is activated. While in the shower I loudly verbalize statements like these:

- I am grateful for my beautiful, hardworking, intelligent son...
- I am grateful for my wife...
- I am grateful for my health...

When I say these things I truly feel them, and visualize them. I don't just say them for the sake of saying them. What this habit does is start my day with grounded optimism and positivity, setting me up for the day with the happiness of knowing I have a good life.

▶▶ 🕐 TIME IN

What are you grateful for? How often do you remember and remind yourself of those things? How often do you tell others you are grateful to have them in your life?

✪ ACTION

To improve your wellbeing create your own gratitude habit and practice it every day.

THE MINDFULNESS HABIT

With our thoughts constantly wandering back and forth between the past and the future, chances are we spend the least amount of our time in the present. Mindfulness is simply a moment-by-moment awareness of what is happening around us, without passing judgment. Being mindful is about being present and, that is more easily said than done.

Some early research on mindfulness was conducted by Ellen Langer, a Professor of psychology at Harvard University. In her book *Mindfulness*, published in 1990, she suggested that mindfulness improves health and overall wellbeing.

As we get older, we were told, our overall health is supposed to get worse. We start losing our vision and hearing, our cognitive abilities will decline, etc. But what if there is a way to reverse this? What if there is a way to improve instead of worsen our overall health? What if there is a way to take ourselves back 20 years and feel as if we were 20 years younger?

This is what Langer wanted to find out. She recruited men between the ages of 75 and 80 and placed them for one week in a beautiful resort that was setup as if it were 1959. The men were asked not to bring anything to the resort that is more recent than 1959.

The newspaper and magazines in the resort were from September 1959. So were the radio shows, announcements and commercials. They watched movies, TV shows and sport events from that period.

The participants were divided into two groups. The researchers told both groups that they believed the stay in this resort would have a positive impact on their lives.

The control group was asked to discuss and remember 1959 in past tense. The experimental group on the other hand was directed to be the person they were in 1959.

Prior to entering the resort, during the stay, and at the end of their stay, participants were video recorded and certain measurements were conducted: physical strength, vision, hearing, cognition, etc. Each participant was photographed before and after their stay.

The results of this research were astonishing. After staying in this resort for only one week, the experimental group's vision, hearing and cognitive ability improved. Their blood pressure dropped. They moved faster and stood taller.

The control group received some great benefits as well. At the end of the say, all the men looked a few years younger and ate and slept better than before.

A study recently presented by the American Heart Association showed that patients who practice mindfulness can reduce their risk of death by half from heart attacks, strokes and other causes when compared to similar patients who were only given an education about healthy living, but did not practice mindfulness.

By practicing mindfulness you truly get to know yourself and the world around you. There are also many side benefits of mindfulness such as feelings of relaxation, reduced stress, help with difficult emotions, and being better able to control anger and other feelings and desires.

In the world we live in, very few of us can dedicate hours to meditation, but we don't have to do that in order to be mindful. We can do so at any time throughout the day and still gain huge benefits.

In his course, *Practicing Mindfulness: An Introduction to Meditation*, Mark W. Muesse explains a number of different mindfulness techniques. Four of these techniques—breathing, walking, eating and driving—I turned into habits. These habits will help you live in the moment and focus on the positive.

Start practicing some of these for just a few minutes, and as you train your brain in these skills, keep steadily extending the time.

Mindful Breathing

Breathing is something that we don't consciously think about very often. Of course we know *how* to breathe, but *mindful breathing* is something else entirely. To breath mindfully, you need to focus on breathing in and breathing out, and think only about your breath.

Mindful Walking

You can practice *mindful walking* when walking from your car to the office, from the parking lot to supermarket, or walking in a park. These walks can be short or long. Regardless, focus on your steps, your body, your breath, the environment and your surroundings. Focus on the moment of being.

Mindful Eating

To *eat mindfully* is to eat slowly, taking your time to eat each and every bite of your meal. Look at the food before you eat it, focus on the shape, smell, texture, color, taste, etc. Think about what was required to produce this food and all the steps necessary to bring it to your table.

Most people don't have the time to mindfully eat at each and every meal, but you can try this practice at least once a week, and see what a difference it makes.

Mindful Driving

You can also practice *mindful driving.* Driving mindfully is not just a good practice, it is the right thing to do to ensure our safety and that of others.

Mindful driving involves paying attention to everything that is in front of you, including the road, other cars, pedestrians, buildings, signals, etc. Listen to the sound of your car, to sounds on the road, watch for signals people give you from ahead and pay attention to both sides of your car (especially if you're driving on a highway and in the middle lane!).

Focus on the moment of driving. Observe other drivers, but pass no judgment. You don't have to react if someone cuts you off. Reacting negatively will inevitably result in anger and will do nothing to ensure that no one will cut you off again.

Just witnessing the moment will make you aware that these things happen, and help you be mindful and enjoy every moment of your life, whatever it brings.

▶▶ 🕐 TIME IN

Think for a moment what mindful living could do for you. When could you practice mindfulness? Which mindful practices could you introduce into your life? Pick one and make a commitment.

⟳ ACTION

Commit to becoming more mindful. Chose one mindful exercise to practice this week. At the end of the week, write down (below) a reflection on that exercise. What worked well? Why? What are you going to do differently based on this experience?

_____

_____

THE MEDITATION HABIT

Meditation is working with your mind to be in the present moment. This moment, the moment you are reading this sentence, is all you have. The past is gone and cannot be changed regardless what you do. The future is not here yet.

Training your brain to be in the present will help you deal with issues like sadness, anger, pain and other difficult life circumstances, when they arrive.

This is not to say that you should always be in the moment and not think about the future. You certainly should make a plan and take action to create a better future for yourselves and others. But constantly worrying about it creates nothing but stress.

Research done at the University of California suggests that focusing on the present, rather than letting the mind drift, helps lower the stress hormone *cortisol*. Less cortisol in our body means we can deal more easily with life circumstances. But how do we focus on the present moment?

Many of us have limiting beliefs about meditation that hold us back from even trying. It was the same for me until I decided to attend the Certificate of Positive Psychology program offered by Dr. Tal Ben-Shahar. While doing breathing exercises, a faculty member, Deborah Cohen, taught me one of the most important lessons of meditation and I finally felt comfortable not just trying, but meditating daily afterwards.

She taught me that regardless of the type of meditation you are doing, *unwanted thoughts* will come to your mind. As long as you are aware of these thoughts you are being mindful and meditating. Observe the thoughts and then return to the chosen focus.

If the same or similar thoughts return, that is okay. Again, as long as you are aware of the returning thoughts, you are being mindful and you are meditating. All you need to do is observe them again and continue your meditation. And just like with anything else in life, the more you practice, the better you become.

There are hundreds of meditative practices that can help you focus on the present. Regardless of the kind you practice, another important fact to keep in mind is that *there is no right or wrong way of meditating.*

The mindful eating, walking, and breathing habits we discussed earlier are types of meditation. There, we focused on the object (eating, walking, and breathing). Since the activity can be considered meditation, we can mindfully focus on any daily activity.

In her book *How to Meditate: A Practical Guide to Making Friends with your Mind,* Pema Chodron recommends meditating during your daily activities such as brushing your teeth. That becomes the focus of your attention.

Chodron recommends you say to yourself: "This is going to be a meditation period, and my attention is to stay present as I'm brushing my teeth. When my attention wanders, I'm going to bring it back to brushing my teeth".

To make it even more powerful, combine this meditation habit with what we learned earlier in this book—brush your teeth with a non-dominant hand. This way you will improve your willpower and start a new meditation habit at the same time.

▶▶ 🕐 TIME IN

Think about what you can do to introduce some kind of meditative practice into your life. How can you train your mind to lower your stress level and improve your wellbeing?

↺ ACTION

Meditate five to ten minutes every day.

THE WALKING HABIT

I have a friend in his late 50s who has always managed to stay slim, and I was curious about what his secret was. When he told me he didn't exercise I was particularly surprised and wanted to know more.

It turns out that he always takes a walk after lunch and dinner and has been doing so for years. He is also careful about his meal portions, which is something many of us can benefit from. Furthermore, he always ensures there is at least a two hour gap between his last meal of the day and when he goes to bed.

These are all habits that he implemented years ago, and it is clear they work well for him. So I decided to implement a "take a walk after dinner" habit. This is a habit that does not require any specific conditions to be met. Anyone can do this whenever they feel.

Keeping up this habit made me keen to get home from work earlier so that I would have enough time to go for a quick walk after dinner. Finding an accountability partner was also a key for me, and therefore my wife and I both decided to adopt this habit.

We started taking short walks of 10 to 15 minutes, but later on these walks became longer, particularly when this was especially necessary, such as after a more generous dinner.

As with any habit, understanding what the triggers are is especially helpful. In this case the trigger was very simple – eating dinner triggered going out for a walk. My rewards for developing this habit were many: I was keeping myself in good shape and benefitting my long-term health, and I was getting one-on-one time with my wife without any distractions, helping us to stay connected.

▶▶ ⏱ TIME IN

What do you do immediately after lunch? What about after dinner? Should you change that habit? If so make a commitment.

⟳ ACTION

Today, after your meal, take a walk for as little as two minutes. The following day walk for three minutes. Keep doing this every day and increase the time slowly. Remember Just Keep Starting.

THE NEW TV HABIT

How about replacing the habit of watching TV with something else that you've always wanted to do?

After a hard day at work, most people like to get home and relax. For some, this means watching TV until bedtime. If this makes you happy, that's fine.

This is exactly what I used to do every day. I would get home, and no matter what time it was, I would turn on the TV, sit down, and watch it until I was tired. Often I would switch through the hundreds of available channels and find nothing interesting, yet settle for something I didn't really want to watch and still sit in front of the TV anyway.

However, when I realized that I wanted to spend more time focusing on more productive things such as studying, and writing a book, I noticed that I simply didn't have time for TV.

This is a common situation. We would like to do something new but we claim we don't have the time.

If you have a strong enough reason and desire to do something, you will find the time. I simply replaced my TV habit with a new one and now I read instead.

If you want to stop watching TV daily and use that time to implement something new in your life, try this:

First hide the remote control—put it in another room, as far from the TV as possible. This way it will not be as convenient to turn on the TV.

Afterwards, if possible, go to a room that does not have a TV and do whatever else you've wanted to do but never had time for.

To avoid returning to the television, make sure you take everything you want with you. Make sure that there's no reason to come back to whichever room the TV is located in.

If you're tempted to go to the TV room, find any reason you can to distract yourself from turning the TV on—do something else for 15 minutes, and chances are that your brain will forget that you wanted to watch TV. The creation of new habits in a new environment and new surroundings will make it much easier to start developing your new habit.

In my case I was replacing my *watching TV habit* with a *reading habit*. To make it easier for myself, I placed the book that I wanted to read right next to my bed, so that as soon as I lay down, the book was within reach.

If I ever felt an urge to go and watch TV again, I simply didn't do it. My old habit would try to kick in, but instead of following it I would focus on establishing the new one.

▸▸🕐 TIME IN

How much time do you spend in front of the TV? Is that time well spent? Should you cut down on that time and do something else instead?

↻ ACTION

List all the activities that you want to do but don't have the time to do. Identify the day/time that you can cut from watching TV and use that time to work on the things you did not have the time for until now. Make it a habit. Have fun!

THE JOURNALING HABIT

Journaling is the practice of keeping a daily dairy of life events. Research by James W. Pennebaker, Professor of psychology at the University of Texas shows that writing is actually therapeutic and good for our health. But just how long we need to write to gain these benefits is still something of an open question.

More recent work done by Laura A. King from the University of Missouri and Chad M. Burton, from the University of Pittsburgh, shows that even journaling for two minutes a day for two days improves well being.

In a lab environment, participants wrote for two minutes a day, two days in a row. They were randomly assigned to write about trauma, positive experiences, or a controlled topic that did not involve many emotions. Before and after each writing session participants filled out a questionnaire about their moods.

Four to six weeks later, researches sent a follow up mood survey. They found that the participants who wrote about trauma or a positive experience had improved wellbeings overall.

Does this mean that all it took for participants to improve their health was two minutes of writing about a positive or a traumatic experience? Probably not. Chances are, after they finished the writing, participants kept thinking about their experience for some time. The writing is what triggered their thinking.

Knowing this research, I decided to give journaling a try. I made it easy for myself to establish this new habit. I put my journal next to my bed with a pen. To minimize any chance of distraction, I made sure I had two pens in case one run out of ink.

I also decided to only journal for two minutes, partly because of the experiment and partly because that would give me no excuse not to do it. That by itself contributed to the successful implementation of the habit. I also determined that the time for my journaling would always be right before going to sleep.

There is one more important fact. My journaling focus was only on three good things that happened that day. This helped me focus on what went well rather than what did not, and put me in a good mood right before going to sleep.

Now that you know that you can improve your health and wellbeing just by journaling for two minutes a day, don't you think it's worth a try? I suggest challenging yourself to try journaling for two minutes for 30 days and see where it takes you. Personally, it took me to a much better place, made me a better person, and brought me to writing this book.

▶▶⏱ TIME IN

Is journaling something you think you could introduce into your daily routine? Could you commit two minutes a day to this habit? Give it a try and see where it takes you.

⟳ ACTION

Make a commitment to journal for at least two days.

Here is a sample form you can use to write about three good things that happened today.

Day	Journaling – Positive Experience
Day 1	
Day 2	

THE UNEXPECTED KINDNESS HABIT

We like people who are kind to us. If we are kind, chances are we will be liked as well. Helping others and being kind is the morally right thing to do. Research shows that in being kind, you not only help others, but also yourself—it improves your overall happiness level.

While writing in my daily journal I focus on certain themes, one of which is *unexpected kindnesses*. These are nice things I do for others. I called it unexpected kindness because these acts are not expected by others.

Research conducted in 2004 by Sonja Lyubomirsky shows that increasing kindness (doing more than one would normally do) elevates happiness. In this study she asked participants to perform five acts of kindness every week for six weeks.

Participants had the option of doing all six acts in one day or spreading them out throughout the week. These were generally described as things that would benefit others (i.e. writing a thank you note to a former Professor, donating blood, helping a colleague, visiting relatives, etc.)

The participants who spread these acts throughout the week did not increase their happiness level. Why? As Lyubomirsky points out, many of these acts are small, and some people do them anyway on a daily basis, so spreading them through seven days may have made them indistinguishable from regular behavior.

On the other hand, the participants who decided to do these acts all in one day experienced a significant increase in happiness and wellbeing.

Acts of kindness make us feel good, more confident and in control. For me, such acts include giving up my seat on the train, letting other cars go in front of me, cutting flowers from the garden for my wife, helping out my neighbor, and so on.

Being intentionally kind puts me into a good mood, knowing I've put a smile on someone else's face. I know that these small acts of kindness in my life have contributed to my overall level of happiness.

Treat yourself with unexpected kindness towards others and you will become even happier.

⏱ TIME IN

Think of the last time you did something nice and unexpected for someone. How did it make you feel? What is it about that act that makes you still remember it? Make a commitment to do even more of it.

⟡ ACTION

Make a commitment to perform unexpected acts of kindness every week for six weeks. The following are a few ideas: hold the door open for someone, read to a child, write a letter to a teacher or someone special in your life, donate clothes, donate blood, give up a seat on the train, volunteer for seniors, etc.

Day	Unexpected Kindness (Description)
Week 1	
Week 2	
Week 3	
Week 4	
Week 5	
Week 6	

THE BUYING
EXPERIENCE HABIT

Think about an item you bought yourself like clothes, electronics, your first car, a house, etc. It made you happy—probably very happy—at the time of purchase.

Some of us, when we feel sad, go out and buy something thinking it will make us happy. Other times we simply buy things we'd like to have and at the moment that makes us happy. However, after a while, we get used to the item and forget how happy we were at the time of purchase.

This is not to say that we don't need to purchase things but rather to focus more on purchasing experiences.

A number of studies find a direct positive correlation between income and subjective wellbeing—our wellbeing increases with the money we have. It is no surprise that money increases wellbeing. But what else can we do with money, after we satisfy our basic needs, to improve our wellbeing?

Professor Ryan Howell from San Francisco State University recruited more than 1,400 people to participate in his research. Participants were asked to complete a questionnaire that measures income, life satisfaction, financial security, credit card debt, etc.

This research shows that what really matters for our long-lasting happiness and financial wellbeing is buying experiences and not buying things. It suggests that our spending choices, and not our absolute income, affects our wellbeing.

Experiences can be little things like having lunch with a friend, colleague, or partner, or going to the theater, on a vacation, etc. The key is to make it a habit.

Buying experiences instead of buying things will bring you long-lasting happiness. The memory from purchasing items fades over time while the memory of enjoying time with your friends and family lasts a very long time.

I tell anyone who wishes to buy me a present to buy me an experience instead, and I also make clear that the experience I am looking for could cost nothing. They can invite me to take a walk together in the park, play some sports, watch a movie at home, or simply get together and enjoy each other's company.

Last year when my son asked me what I wanted for Christmas, I suggested he buy me an experience. He made a lunch reservation in an Italian restaurant in Manhattan and my wife, my son, and his girlfriend had a really great time.

The image of this lunch experience is still beautifully painted in my mind and will be there for years to come.

▶▶ 🕐 TIME IN

How can you buy more experiences for yourself and others? What experience habit can you commit to right now? Go ahead, buy that experience and improve your happiness and overall wellbeing.

◈ ACTION

Identify an experience you can buy immediately for yourselves and others.

On the next page, name 12 experiences, one for each month, that you can buy for yourself and others. Mark YES when completed.

Month	Experience	Completed	
		YES	NO
January			
February			
March			
April			
May			
June			
July			
August			
September			
October			
November			
December			

THE SPENDING MONEY WELL HABIT

Can you really establish a habit of buying wellbeing? This may sound far-fetched, but research clearly shows you can.

What would you do if you were given some money and asked to spend it that day? What would make you happier—spending it on yourself or others?

That is exactly what Elizabeth W. Dunn, Associate Professor of psychology at University of British Columbia, Lara B. Aknin, Assistant Professor of psychology at Simon Fraser University, and Michael I. Norton, Associate Professor of business administration at Harvard University, wanted to find out. They gathered a group of students and gave them money randomly—to some they gave $5 and others they gave $20.

They told the students that the money was theirs and to spend it anyway they wanted, but they needed to spend it by the end of the day. They could buy things for themselves or spend it on others. Before receiving the money, and at the end of the day (after spending the money) the participants filled out questionnaires that allowed the researchers to measure their happiness level.

Participants also reported how they spent their money. For those who spent the money on themselves, they mostly purchased magazines, school suppliers and food. Those who spent the money on other people mostly purchased toys for siblings, meals for the homeless or shared a meal with a friend.

It turned out that participants who spent the money on others ended the day much happier than the participants who decided to spend the money on themselves. It is also interesting to notice that the amount of money did not matter—the results were about the same regardless of whether they received $5 or $20. The only thing that mattered is how they spent the money. Regardless of the amount of money they spent, the people who spent money on others were happier.

▶▶⏱ TIME IN

How can you improve your happiness level based on this research? What can you do today to make it happen?

↻ ACTION

Make a habit to buy your own happiness. It's simple. Buy a present for others. Give money to charity. Do some volunteering. Buy a present for someone else.

THE SMILE HABIT

Many of us may have been told that we should smile more often. Studies suggest that smiling has multiple benefits on our wellbeing. But what if we fake a smile to purposefully introduce health benefits to our life? Is that possible?

That is one thing that Tara Kraft and Sarah Pressman, Professors of psychology from the University of Kansas, researched in 2011. However, as usual, the study participants were told something else—the purpose of the study was how multitasking affects performance ability.

They recruited 170 participants for the study. The researchers asked them to perform two stressful tasks while holding pencils in their mouths. Heart rate and breathing was recorded by electrodes placed on the participants. Blood pressure was recorded as well.

The participants were assigned to groups with directions to hold the pencil between their teeth while smiling, frowning, or having a neutral expression.

All the smiling participants had lower heart rates and reduced stress during the recovery than the neutral group. The research suggests that maintaining a positive facial expression has both physiological and psychological benefits.

In addition to stress reduction, according to the Mayo Clinic, other benefits of smiling are an improved immune system, pain relief and greater personal satisfaction.

Also, when we smile, we trick our brain into thinking we are happy. When our brain thinks we are happy, it releases dopamine, the "happy chemical."

Shawn Achor recommends that we smile three extra times a day. By that he means that in addition to our daily smiles, we should smile in situations that we do not normally smile, such as in meetings, during a sales pitch, etc.

According to Achor's research, this one small change can create a huge return on investment such as raising your social and emotional intelligence and improving your mood. We can all benefit in many ways from creating the smile habit. It is free and simple.

The Waking Up With a Smile Habit

The way we start our day defines it. Most of us have heard the expression "Did you get up on the wrong side of the bed?", and most of us have had days where we feel and act like we did.

But the fact of the matter is that we decide whether we want to be happy in the morning or not. It may sound strange to some, but it's true. We sometimes decide that we want to be unhappy in the morning because we have to go to work, because we did not get enough sleep, because our financial situation is not as we would like it to be, or any other number of reasons.

Research done by Robert Zajonc from the University of Michigan shows that facial expressions are a biological reaction that alters our blood as well as the temperature in our brain. So just making that smile, even if we don't really have a reason to smile or even don't want to smile, will create a biological reaction in our body. What a powerful tool we now have at our disposal!

To help myself wake up on the right side of the bed, I schedule a smile every morning. It is scheduled right before I go to sleep and delivered at 5 AM every day. As soon as I hear my alarm, I smile, and keep it for a while. Whether I'm feeling happy or not, when I hear that alarm clock, I smile.

Let's smile!

▶▶ ⏲ TIME IN

Do you think you smile enough?

What's the first thing you do when you wake up? Are you upset? Angry? Happy? How would you like to feel as soon as you wake up? Think about what you need to do in order to have that feeling that will keep you going all day long.

⟳ ACTION

If smiling is not your habit already, work on it. Make it a habit. Make it a habit to smile as soon as you wake up regardless of how you feel. This will enable your brain to help you have a good—if not great—day.

THE REPLACEMENT HABIT

In Chapter One I explained that the habits we create are always there and can never be deleted. The best way to stop carrying out the *unwanted habit* is to replace it with a new *wanted habit*.

I applied this knowledge to replace my bad habit of drinking soda with the good habit of drinking water. Here is how I did it.

First I analyzed my habit and noticed that on the weekend, I would go outside to my yard, start doing some work, and every once in a while, go to the garage, open up the fridge and get a soda. I was aware that this was not a healthy choice but I still kept doing it.

I also knew this habit had been solidly engraved in my brain for years, and if I wanted to change it, I needed to make it as easy as possible on my brain to make that change.

In order to do that I kept many elements of the old habit: while working outside on the weekends, when I got tired and sweaty, I would go to the garage, open up the fridge and get a drink. The only difference was that this time I would take water instead of soda.

To make it easier for me to implement this new habit, I made sure there was no soda in the fridge and that bottles of water were waiting for me in the same spot I used to have soda.

Consider trying a similar trick on some of your habits that you want to change for the better.

▶▶🕐 TIME IN

Do you have a habit involving a reward that is ultimately bad for you? Could you keep many elements of the habit but change the reward? If so, make a commitment and start working on it.

⟳ ACTION

List some of your bad habits and think about how you can apply the knowledge from Chapter One and The Replacement Habit to replace bad habits with good habits. Use as many old habit elements as possible to help you make this happen.

Bad Old Habit	Good New Habit
1.	
2.	
3.	
4.	
5.	
6.	

THE YOGA HABIT

Yoga has been known and practiced for hundreds of years and practitioners receive numerous benefits from it. In addition to its health benefits, since practicing yoga can increase control over your mind, it can also help you overcome your bad habits and introduce new ones.

Research on the benefits of yoga is still relatively new. Work done by the Institute for Extraordinary Living (IEL) over the past seven years shows that yoga reduces stress and anxiety, reduces anger in high school students, decreases negativity, improves wellbeing, and even shows potential results in dealing with post-traumatic stress disorder.

Today, there are many places we can go to learn yoga. The problem with most of us who have an extremely busy life is finding the time to do that. The issue is how to get started.

If you can find the time, one way to learn about it is to go a yoga retreat center. This would give you time to experience it firsthand and therefore make it easier to establish your own yoga routine when you come back home.

The other way is to find a local yoga center just to get you started and see if it is something you would like to implement as a new habit. But probably the most likely way to start is to begin practicing it at home.

Following the *Small Wins Habit* I recommend you start like I did. If you are not regular practitioner, and still not sure if this is something you want to dedicate a lot of time to, then five minutes or so a day will be a great start.

Certainly many yoga practitioners will say that five minutes of practicing yoga is not enough, and I agree with them. However, just like with any other habit, the main point is to get started and later on decide how much time you really want to dedicate to this practice. I still practice only five minutes or so a day and that is good enough for me.

To get started practicing at home, find some free online program. You will find many videos that are five or so minutes in length. As with any other habits, it is best that you schedule a specific time to do it and follow the same timeframe throughout your practice.

For me, the best time is in the morning, once I am done with my breathing exercise—which becomes a trigger for my yoga break. In addition, I practice during the day whenever I find it appropriate.

▶▶🕐 TIME IN

Think about the benefits of yoga. If you are not a practitioner already, would you consider giving it a try? If so, what is the best day/time for you to implement this habit?

THE NATURE HABIT

We know that spending time in nature is good for us and yet some of us don't do it and others don't do it enough. In today's world, it is easy to get distracted by watching TV, enjoying our favorite electronic gadgets, or spending time on the internet and social networking sites.

This is not to say that technology should not have a place in our lives. However, we should not ignore that our bodies and our minds have other important needs in order to stay healthy and happy.

Research performed in 2012 by Peter Aspinall, Panagiotis Mavros, Richard Coyne and Jenny Roe suggests that people who spend time in green space showed evidence of lower frustration and higher meditation state.

In their study, participants were asked to walk for 25 minutes through three different areas (zone 1—urban shopping streets, zone 2—

through green space, and zone 3—a very busy commercial district). They traveled individually through all three zones while being followed by researchers. The organizers measured four predictors (frustration, engagement, alertness, and meditation) via 14 sensors positioned on the participants' scalps using emotional based recognition software.

The researchers measured changes when people moved from one zone to another. They found that when participants moved from zone 1 to zone 2 (urban shopping to green spaces) they showed reduction in three out of four predictors (frustration, engagement and alertness) and increase in meditation. When moving from zone 2 to zone 3 (green space to busy commercial district) engagement and alertness dominated.

I used to hike for hours to get to green spaces, reach mountains and enjoy the scenery. But we don't need to do this in order to benefit from nature. Regardless of where we live, chances are there is a park or park-like environment close to us.

In addition, many of us work in areas called office parks. Some businesses invest a lot of money to build these park-like environments so that we can relax, minimize stress and focus more on our work when we go back to our offices.

Ideally, once you establish a habit of spending time in nature, you can combine other habits such as breathing and mindfulness. There is no better place to practice these habits than in nature.

Enjoying nature once a week or even once a month will improve your health and help you focus on other things in your life that are important.

▶▶ 🕐 TIME IN

Do you have green space near where you live or work? Can you spend more time outside? How often can you go out during business hours?

♢ ACTION

Establish a habit (every day, week, month) to go to a park or other green space, to relax and enjoy the moment. Spend some time alone there to have a chance to do some breathing and meditation practices at the same time.

THE STRENGTH AT WORK HABIT

Most of us grew up in a culture where work was supposed to be something we just did to pay our bills. Based on that definition, joy and fun happens outside of work. Because of this belief we are often stressed, unhappy, unhealthy and certainly less productive.

Do you like your job? Unfortunately for many people the answer is no. If you really don't like your job then following your passion and finding your calling might be one answer, but that is not what I am talking about here.

I am referring to using your strengths at work regardless of whether or not you like your job. By doing so, you will increase your happiness level, improve wellbeing, boost productivity and possibly turn your job into a career.

In his book *Curious?*, Dr. Todd Kashdan, Professor of psychology at George Mason University, goes much deeper into this idea. He suggests that we need to infuse work with more meaning and the best way to do that is first discover our strengths and then bring them into the workplace.

While discovering my strengths, I realized that I am what Dr. Todd Kashdan calls a *curious explorer*, someone whose top character strength is curiosity. The following are a few habit examples of how I apply this strength.

Even before I get to work, I have certain *strength habits* to get me started. As I drive to work, I attempt to use different roads. By doing so I apply my strength, practice mindfulness, and learn about my surroundings. When I stop to get gas I ask questions and learn about the person who is pumping the gas in my car.

As soon as I get to work, I want to learn what happened during the night (since I am responsible for a 24-hour production environment). Then I get a coffee and find people in the break room to talk to. They tell me about their family, kids, and about the good things going on in their lives.

Once I apply my strength and feel good about my day, I am ready to take care of any task. I know that applying my curiosity strength will give me fuel to be even more productive at work.

▶▶🕐 TIME IN

Think of your strengths. What are you really good at? How can you do more of it? In what environment and circumstances can you feel comfortable applying this strength?

↔ ACTION

Get your free character strength profile from VIA Institute (viacharacter.org). Find your top five strengths. Apply them consistently every day. Notice the difference in your career wellbeing.

THE MONEY
MANAGEMENT HABIT

Based on a research done by the Gallup organization and data from more than 150 countries, one of the major categories of living a good life is financial wellbeing. So far we have covered two major Gallup recommendations to improve our financial wellbeing: *Buy Experiences* and *Spend Money on Others*.

These habits require having some money. This financial habit may not necessarily help you make more money, but it will certainly help you understand your finances and therefore give you the option to change some of your possibly bad financial patterns.

Regardless of how much money you make, chances are that you have multiple financial accounts; a mortgage, some credit cards, a checking, saving or retirement account, department store credit cards, etc. So what habit will help you improve your financial wellbeing? I simply call it *Money Management.*

The secret to financial wellbeing is not how much you make, but how well you manage your money. Entering data and controlling your finances is one thing. Establishing a habit to deeply analyze it on an ongoing basis is another. And this is a habit I am talking about here.

Years ago I tried to establish this habit and it was very difficult. And since it required an extremely high number of hours on a weekly basis, I gave up.

Then about four years ago, I learned about a free personal finance service/software (multiple free internet services are available today) that helped me establish and maintain this habit. It will not make money for me, nor will it make any financial decisions for me, but as long as I review the results on a weekly basis, it can save me a lot of money, and more importantly, it gives me my full financial picture.

In addition to saving money, I also have a very good picture on what I spend on a monthly or yearly basis, what my budget is, and what my overall financial obligations are. The program warns me if I do not save enough and warns that this could move up my scheduled retirement date.

Overall, this habit takes a long time to establish, since you need to invest the time to set up all of your accounts, but once you do it, all it takes is the regular routine of looking at the analysis and taking action based on that. You will be surprised how much you spend on certain categories, and your potential savings.

This habit will certainly help you understand your other spending habits. Once you see the results of the analysis, it will be up to you to decide if you want to change your spending habits or not.

▶▶⏰ TIME IN

Think for a moment about your finances. Do you know how much you spend each month on credit card and bank fees? Groceries? What financial goals do you have? Are they in line with your income and expenses? When can you retire?

↻ ACTION

Find a tool that will help you manage your finances. Dedicate the time to enter the data, connect all your income and expense accounts, enter your goals, etc. Review the analysis and take appropriate actions when necessary.

THE REMINDER HABIT

Although we covered many habits in this book and a lot of material necessary to understand and change our habits, if you are working on establishing even one new habit, congratulations! I know it is not easy. You are the one doing the work and I am just here to support you.

But how do you constantly remind yourself to perform a habit you want to establish? It sounds simple, but it is not. It is almost like you need to develop a habit to remind yourself about the habit you want to develop.

Before any task becomes a habit or a ritual, we need to work hard to get there and we need to use all the tools available to help us get there.

You can use objects you already have and wear every day such as a watch, cell phone, jewelry etc. as your reminder. Here is an example.

Let's say you want to remind yourself about the *Five Deep Breaths* exercise and you want to do this at least few times a day. If you have a watch you can use it as a reminder. Every time you look at your watch, in addition to getting to know the time, it will serve as a reminder to do this exercise. Your watch in this example will serve as a reminder for your breathing exercise.

You can also purchase a special bracelet to serve as a reminder for specific habit. Let's say you want to be calm while driving. The bracelet will be a constant reminder to calm down, and drive mindfully.

After 30 days, you may begin to truly drive mindfully. You can then use the same bracelet to focus on a new habit.

Let's say you want to eat slowly and begin truly enjoying your food. After a certain period of time, once you feel comfortable using this bracelet as a reminder for eating slowly, you can now switch and use the same bracelet as a reminder to focus on your listening skills. As you can see, one object can help with multiple habits.

Certain objects placed outside on the street can also serve as reminders. For example, every time you see a STOP sign, it can serve as a reminder that you need to slow down (and of course make a full stop)—even if just for a moment. Take a deep breath.

You can also place some reminders to serve as a habit triggers. For example, if you want to implement a journaling habit, you can place your journal on top of your pillow, so that when you go to sleep, you can't miss the journaling.

If you want to implement a habit of weighing yourself every morning, place the scales right next to your bathtub. After you take a shower, the scales will remind you to implement your daily weighing habit.

Use reminders to help you remember the habits you want to implement. Remember that a reminder can be anything—from the watch you wear every day, to a STOP sign.

⏱ TIME IN

Pick a habit you are working on. What can serve as a reminder? Pick another habit. Identify a reminder.

⟳ ACTION

List all of the new habits and identify reminders for each one.

Habit	Reminder
1.	
2.	
3.	
4.	
5.	
6.	
7.	
8.	
9.	
10.	

Now this is not the end. It is not even the beginning of the end. But it is, perhaps, the end of the beginning.

– Winston Churchill

CONCLUSION

I am truly grateful that you joined me in this habits journey. As Mr. Churchill said, it is the end of the beginning—but we know there is no end to our habits.

Now that you have basic knowledge about habits and perhaps implemented new and replaced some old ones, what's next?

Let's continue this journey together. I would love to hear from you and see how I can help even more to assure you implement this knowledge the best you can. Please feel free to connect with me on facebook at www.facebook.com/braco.pobric, visit my website at www.HabitsAndHappiness. com or reach out to me via my email at Braco@ HabitsAndHappiness.com. I would be honored to hear from you and more than happy to help you on your new habit journey.

REFERENCES

Achor S. (2010). *The Happiness Advantage: The Seven Principles of Positive Psychology That Fuel Success and Performance at Work.* Crown Business.

_____. (2013). *Before Happiness: The 5 Hidden Keys to Achieving Success, Spreading Happiness, and Sustaining Positive Change.* Crown Business.

Allen D. (2002). *Getting Things Done: The Art of Stress-Free Productivity.* Penguin Books.

Aspinall, P.,Mavros P., Coyne, R. and Roe. J. (2013). *The urban brain: analyzing outdoor physical activity with mobile EEG.* School of Built Environment, Heriot-Watt University, Edinburgh, UK.

Baumeister R.F., Tierney J. (2012). *Willpower: Rediscovering the Greatest Human Strength.* Penguin Books.

Ben-Shahar, T. (2010). *Being Happy: You Don't Have to be Perfect to Lead a Richer, Happier Life.* McGraw-Hill.

_____. (2012). *Choose the Life You Want: 101 Ways to Create Your Own Road to Happiness.* The Experiment.

_____. (2007). *Happier: Learn the Secrets to Daily Joy and Lasting Fulfillment.* McGraw-Hill.

Burchard B. (2012). *The Charge: Activating the 10 Human Drives That Make You Feel Alive.* Free Press.

Burton, C. M. and King, L. A. (2008). *Effects of (Very) Brief Writing on Health: The Two-Minute Miracle.* British Journal of Health Psychology 13 (2008): 9–14.

Chodron, P. (2013). *How to Meditate: A Practical Guide to Making Friends with Your Mind.* Sounds True.

Cope S. (2012). *Yoga Research at Kripalu: The Power of Possibility.* Kripalu Center for Yoga & Health.

Crum T. and Hansen M.V. (2009). *Three Deep Breaths: Finding Power and Purpose in a Stressed-Out World.* Berrett-Koehler Publishers.

Csikszentmihalyi M. (1998). *Finding Flow: The Psychology of Engagement with Everyday Life.* Basic Books.

Doidge N. (2007). *The Brain That Changes Itself: Stories of Personal Triumph from the Frontiers of Brain Science.* Penguin Books.

Duhigg C. (2012). *The Power of Habit: Why We Do What We Do in Life and Business.* Random House.

Dweck C. (2007). *Mindset: The New Psychology of Success.* Ballantine Books.

Dyer W. D. (2009). *Excuses Begone!: How to Change Lifelong, Self-Defeating Thinking Habits.* Hay House.

_____. (2010). *The Power of Intention: Learning to Co-create Your World Your Way.* Hay House.

_____. (1976). *Your Erroneous Zones: Step-by-Step Advice for Escaping the Trap of Negative Thinking and Taking Control of Your Life.* Funk & Wagnalls.

Fiore N. (2005). *The Now Habit: A Strategic Program for Overcoming Procrastination and Enjoying Guilt-Free Play.* Tarcher.

_____. (2010). *The Now Habit at Work: Perform Optimally, Maintain Focus, and Ignite Motivation in Yourself and Others.* Wiley.

Fredrickson B. (2009). *Positivity: Top-Notch Research Reveals the 3 to 1 Ratio That Will Change Your Life.* Harmony.

Gorin A, Phelan S, Tate D, Sherwood N, Jeffery R, Wing R. (2005). *Involving support partners in obesity treatment.* The Miriam Hospital/Brown Medical School and University of Massachusetts Dartmouth.

Hanson R. (2013). *Hardwiring Happiness: The New Brain Science of Contentment, Calm, and Confidence.* Harmony.

Heath C., Heath D. (2010). *Switch: How to Change Things When Change Is Hard.* Crown Business.

Howell R.T. , Kurai M., Tam L. (2012). *Money buys financial security and psychological need satisfaction: Testing need theory in affluence.* Social Indicators Research: an international and interdisciplinary journal for quality of life measurement, Online first 1-13.

James W. (1914). *Habit.* Henry Holt and Company.

Kabat-Zinn J. (1991). *Full Catastrophe Living: Using the Wisdom of Your Body and Mind to Face Stress, Pain, and Illness.* Dell Pub. Group.

Kashdan T. (2009). *Curious?: Discover the Missing Ingredient to a Fulfilling Life.* William Morrow.

Kawakami, K., Dovidio, J. F. and Dijksterhuis, A. (2003). *Effect of Social Category Priming on Personal Attitudes.* Psychological Science 14 (2003): 315–319.

Kraft L. Tara, Pressman D. Sarah (2012). *Grin and Bear It. The Influence of Manipulated Facial Expression on the Stress Response.* Psychological Science.

Langer J. E. (1989). *Mindfulness.* Da Capo Press.

Lipton B. (2005). *The Biology of Belief: Unleashing the Power of Consciousness, Matter & Miracles.* Hay House.

Loehr J., Schwartz T. (2003). *The Power of Full Engagement: Managing Energy, Not Time, Is the Key to Performance and Personal Renewal.* The Free Press.

Lyubomirsky S.(2007). *The How of Happiness: A New Approach to Getting the Life You Want.* Penguin Books.

Muesse W. Mark (2011). *Practicing Mindfulness: An Introduction to Meditation.* The Great Courses.

Parthasarath A. (2009). *Vedanta Treatise The Eternities.* Vedanta Life Institute.

Pennebaker W. J. (1997). *Writing about Emotional Experiences as a Therapeutic Process.* Psychological Science. San Francisco State University and Old Dominion University.

Peterson, G., D.B. Abrams, et al. (1985). *Professional Versus Self-Help Weight Loss at the Worksite: The Challenge of Making a Public Health Impact.* Behavior Therapy 16: 213-222.

Phillips O. , Denning M. *Practical Guide to Creative Visualization: Manifest Your Desires*. Llewellyn Publication.

Rath T. (2013). *Eat Move Sleep: How Small Choices Lead to Big Changes*. Missionday.

_____. (2007). *StrengthsFinder 2.0*. Gallup Press.

Rath T., Harter J. (2010). *Wellbeing: The Five Essential Elements*. Gallup Press.

Ray R. (2006). Documentary Film *10 Questions for the Dalai Lama*. Rick Ray Films.

Rubin G. (2011). *The Happiness Project: Or, Why I Spent a Year Trying to Sing in the Morning, Clean My Closets, Fight Right, Read Aristotle, and Generally Have More Fun*. Harper Paperbacks.

Sarno J.(2010). *Healing Back Pain: The Mind-Body Connection*. Warner Books.

_____.(2007). *The Divided Mind: The Epidemic of Mindbody Disorders*. HarperCollins.

Schreiber S. D. (2004). *The Instinct to Heal: Curing Depression, Anxiety and Stress Without Drugs and Without Talk Therapy*. Rodale Books.

Seligman, M. E. P. (2004). *Authentic Happiness: Using the New Positive Psychology to Realize Your Potential for Lasting Fulfillment*. Free Press.

_____. (1990). *Learned Optimism: How to Change Your Mind and Your Life*. Pocket Books.

Shaw J. (2004). *The Deadliest Sin: From Survival of the Fittest to Staying Fit Just to Survive*. Harvard Magazine.

Verplanken B. and Wood W. (2006). Interventions to Break and Create Consumer . *Journal of Public Policy and Marketing*.

Weick E. K.(1984). *Small wins: Redefining the scale of social problems*. American Psychologist, Vol 39(1).

Wong S. (2010). *The Neuroscience of Everyday Life*. The Teaching Company.

Zajonc B.R. (1985). *Emotion and Facial Efference: A Theory Reclaimed*. University of Michigan.

ACKNOWLEDGMENTS

I would probably never have learned about the science of habits and happiness if it was not for my mom. She taught me a truly practical science of positive psychology decades before the field was officially established, and I am forever grateful to her for that.

There are many people who helped me write this book either directly or indirectly.

Thank you to my dad who taught me to be a strong honest human being, to keep going and to never give up. Thank you to my son Zlatan who helped me write this book and whose dedication to learning and true life success keeps inspiring me.

Thank you to my two sisters: Jasenka, who, when I was a baby, proudly carried her little brother, helped, supported and believed in me all my life, and my sister Jasmina who, when I had a hard time in college, pushed me gently but firmly to assure I graduated.

Thank you to my brother Faruk who protected me and taught me every little secret needed to survive in this world. With his help, I established many habits.

I am extremely thankful to my dear friend and editor Fiona Trembath whose attention to detail and more importantly incredible knowledge of the subject helped me tremendously, but any errors are my own.

Thank you to my colleague, teacher and mentor Tal Ben-Shahar, PhD who supported the writing of this book. Tal's lectures on the science of happiness are reflected in my work. Without his help, this book would still be in its first draft.

My friend and colleague Dr. Maria Siriois's insights found their way into this book. Based on her book publishing experience, she pointed me to the right directions and gave me powerful advice.

I am thankful to my positive psychology, meditation and yoga teacher Debbie Cohen, MAPP. If it was not for Debbie, I would still think that meditation was impossible. Without the breathing and meditation knowledge I received from Debbie, this book would not be the same.

Thank you to my friend and business partner Patrick Howell who inspired me to keep working on this book and always believed in its success.

I have been fortunate enough to have a great supportive family and many friends and colleagues who helped shape my life, habits and therefore this book. I am forever grateful for the support and help I received from them.

This book is dedicated to my wife Nevenka who has been my life partner and a supporter for anything and everything I ever wanted to do. She is a huge believer in me and my works regardless of the circumstances.

I look forward to the new friendships and habits community this book creates.

Thank you all!

ABOUT THE AUTHOR

Braco Pobric is an author, life and executive coach, speaker, educator, and a founding member and Chief Happiness Officer of the Institute for Advanced Human Performance. He is a Certified Positive Psychology Coach and former Certified Trainer and Coach for Dale Carnegie Training.

He currently holds a leadership role with a global financial company. Braco lives in New Jersey with his wife Nevenka and their cat Ringo.

INDEX